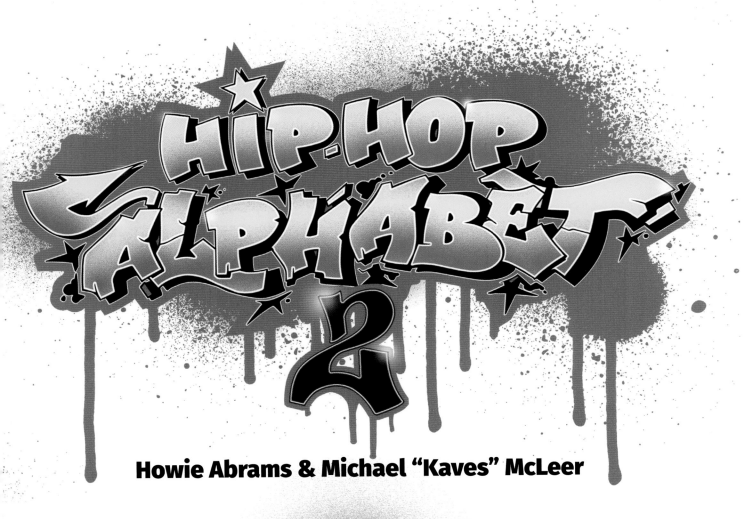

HIP-HOP ALPHABET 2

Howie Abrams & Michael "Kaves" McLeer

PERMUTED
PRESS

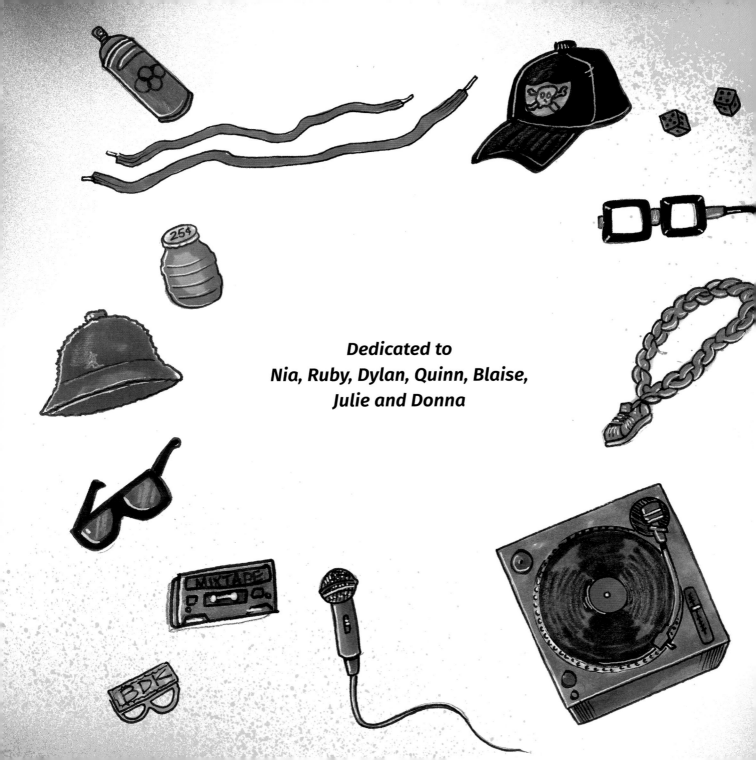

Dedicated to
Nia, Ruby, Dylan, Quinn, Blaise,
Julie and Donna

is for **Action Bronson,**
A colorful rapper who loves to eat.
He's got tattoos, a big red beard,
and fresh jams to move your feet.

OVENFRESH

B is for Breaking.
The original dance of hip-hop
Featured windmills, freezes and headspins,
Popping, locking and Uprock.

is for Chance the Rapper,
An inspiring Chicago emcee.
He mixes gospel and jazz with hot beats,
And on his cap wears the number three.

is for **Dr. Dre**,
A wizard of beats and sound.
He's masterminded many rap classics
and is the most celebrated producer around.

is for **EPMD**,
The slickest duo in the game.
Erick and Parrish always mean business.
Fresh rhymes are their constant aim.

G is for Grandmaster Flash,
A pioneer of turntable style.
He moved his records back and forth,
Keeping bodies moving all the while.

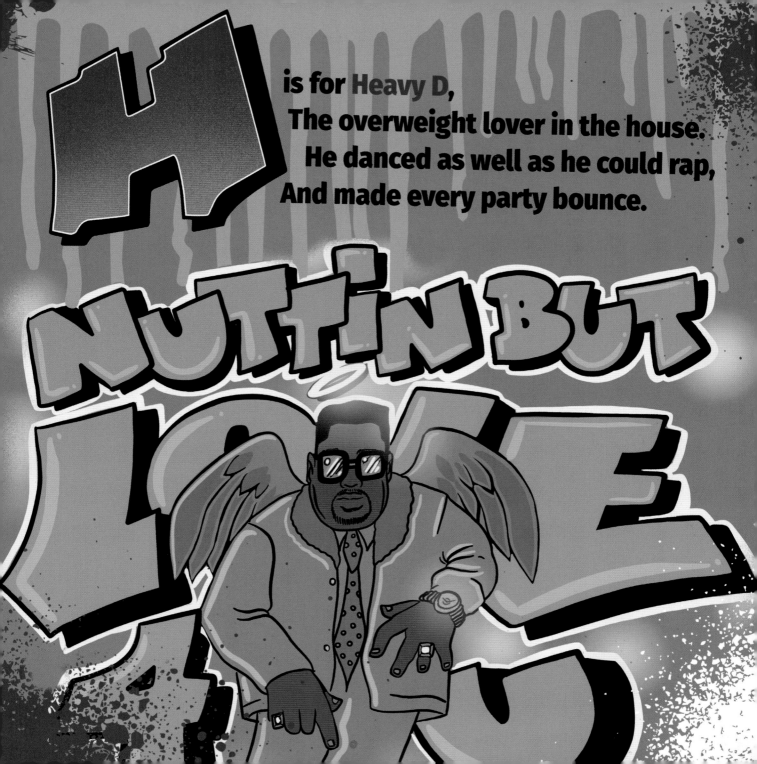

H is for **Heavy D,**
The overweight lover in the house.
He danced as well as he could rap,
And made every party bounce.

J is for Jam Master Jay,
Run DMC's DJ extraordinaire.
Jay made the crowds scream "Hooooo"
And wave their hands in the air.

is for Kendrick Lamar,
Whose rhymes are deep and compelling
His vivid lyrics and distinctive flow
Make him a master of rap storytelling.

is for Lauryn Hill,
A queen in the vocal booth.
She brings rhythm and soul to hip-hop
And always sings the truth.

M is for Missy Elliott,
Who wears the most outrageous attire.
Creativity is her greatest strength,
And her lyrics are always fire.

N is for Nas.
From Queensbridge Houses he came.
An authentic voice for the people,
He's the most poetic lyricist in the game.

NASTY NAS

QUEENSBRIDGE
- NORTH HOUSES -

O is for O.D.B.,
The clown prince of the Wu-Tang Clan.
His wacky wordplay kept fans smiling
From Staten Island to Japan.

P is for Pharrell Williams,
A maestro of music and style.
His productions are otherworldly,
So happy and versatile.

Q is for Questlove,
who plays drums for the mighty Roots crew.
His jazzy grooves and afro pick
Represent Philly through and through.

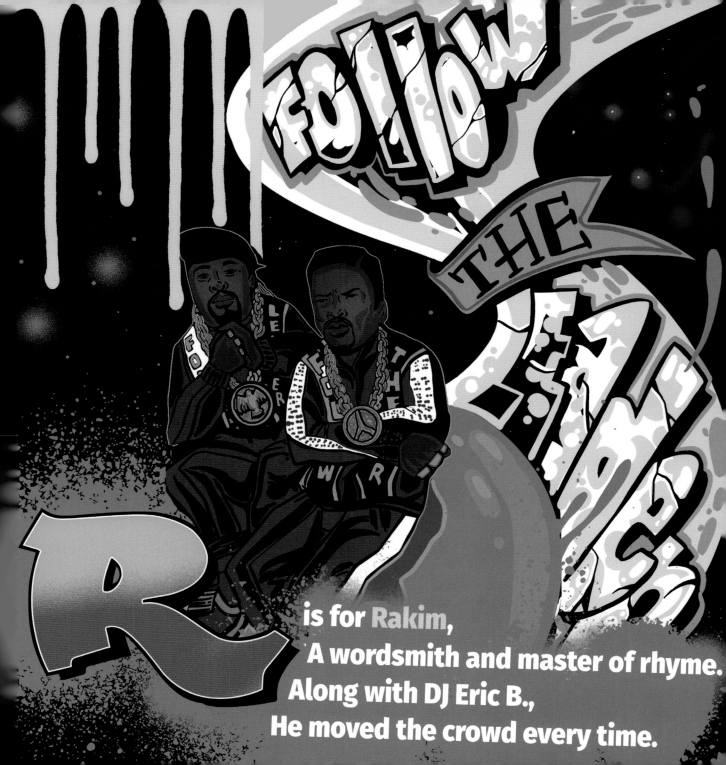

R is for Rakim,
A wordsmith and master of rhyme.
Along with DJ Eric B.,
He moved the crowd every time.

S is for Salt-N-Pepa,
Who sang "Push It" and "Shoop."
They put female rappers on the map
With their dazzling hip-hop troupe.

T is for Tyler the Creator,
The captain of the Odd Future squad.
He skateboards and raps kinda crazy,
With songs called "Smuckers" and "Tron Cat," so odd.

U is for Unorthodox,
And all the rappers who make their own rules,
From Young M.A. to Bumpy Knuckles,
MF Doom and Run the Jewels.

V is for Video Music Box,
The first rap video show.
Hosted by Uncle Ralph in New York,
It keeps hip-hop heads in the know.

VIDEO MUSIC BOX

W is for Wiz Khalifa,
A popular rapper, tall and svelte.
He was born in North Dakota
And is an 8th degree black belt.

X is for X-Clan,
An Afrocentric crew.
From Professor X to Brother J,
They represent their culture in all they do.

Y is for Young MC,
Whose catchy classic, "Bust a Move,"
Can make any party go nuts
To its delicious, funky groove.

Z is for Zephyr,
A king in the graffiti game.
Back in the '80s every subway car
Seemed to bear his name.

ACKNOWLEDGEMENTS

Howie and Kaves would like to thank:

Jacob Hoye and all at Permuted Press, Donna McLeer, Joe Gargano, Nina, Terri and all at the Jam Master Jay Foundation for Music, Andrew "Zephyr" Witten, Rich DiBernardo, plus everyone who showed love for Hip-Hop Alphabet!

A portion of the proceeds from *Hip-Hop Alphabet* will be donated to the Jam Master Jay Foundation for Music. The foundation operates under the simple premise that regardless of socio-economic status, every child deserves equal access to the arts. The foundation supports the idea that social Justice, Arts and Music (J.A.M.) education should be in every school, in every region of the country, giving children the opportunity to expand their worldview through artistic expression.

www.JamMasterJay.org

ABOUT THE AUTHORS

Howie used to work in the music biz
at record labels and such.
Now he is an author,
who loves his family very much.

Kaves is a legendary graffiti artist
and a renaissance man.
He's toured all around the world
with his Lordz of Brooklyn band.

A PERMUTED PRESS BOOK
ISBN: 978-1-68261-8-455

Illustrations by Kaves
Rhymes by Howie Abrams
Cover and interior design by Donna McLeer
Additional illustrations by Bella Kozyreva
Zephyr handstyle by Zephyr

**PERMUTED
PRESS**

Permuted Press, LLC
New York • Nashville
permutedpress.com

Published in the United States of America
Printed in China